Get That Degree
But First...

You Need Stress
Free
College Planning

Gina M. D'Amore-Nisco

IEC, CSMC, CCWC, CLSC, CRC, CPS

D'Amore-Nisco

Printed in the United States of America
Publication Date - May, 2018
Move Forward Publishing

To Contact Author: gina@positivenextsteps.com
www.positivenextsteps.com

ISBN-10: 0-9985908-0-0
ISBN-13: 978-0-9985908-0-6

D'Amore-Nisco

~DEDICATION~

This book is dedicated to all of the students and families who allowed me to be a part of their college planning journey. I am humbled when I receive feedback stating that I was an integral part in that stage of their life and moving forward.

"As with most things in life, we learn from each other if we choose to listen."- Gina M. D'Amore-Nisco

D'Amore-Nisco

CONTENTS

"Everyone has a purpose and a passion. Find yours and live it."- Gina M. D'Amore-Nisco

D'Amore-Nisco

ACKNOWLEDGMENTS

I wish to acknowledge and thank all the college graduates; ***Robert N., Lauren P., Daniel D., Kayla R., Jeremy E., Lauren S., John M., Dara G., Christian G.,*** and ***Lorenzo S.***, who took the time out of their busy lives to compile their thoughts in order to give other students advice for the college years and beyond. It is my hope that their life messages will inspire you as you enter this journey that they have already completed.

Cover picture is my daughter, **Brittany Nisco, receiving her Bachelor's Degree from Western Connecticut State University. A very proud day.

Testimonials

"We were very fortunate to work with Gina when our daughter started the college application process. Gina has a very good understanding about the college process and what the admissions officers are looking for. It was apparent that she was very respected in her field.

The college application process can be very stressful but Gina was able to reduce our stress and navigate us through the process. She has a unique ability to overcome obstacles and always see things in a positive way.

There is a lot of competition to get into the number one school of your choice and Gina was able to present our daughter's strengths as an asset to the school. She worked closely with my daughter and was always accessible to answer our questions.

Gina was a huge asset to us in the college selection process. We were both blessed and honored to have her in our corner. We highly recommend her to any family entering into the college application process."
~Todd & Terry

"I can't tell you how relieved we were to have Gina work with our son. She not only motivated him but made the entire college process stress free. Worth every penny!"
~Rick

"We were lost in a mountain of paperwork and missed deadlines. Finally called Positive Next Steps and Gina took over. She is very knowledgeable and made the transition very smooth. Wish we called her sooner!"
~Patty

"Gina is so consistent and thorough in everything she does. I've never met anyone as persistent and dedicated as her. She truly cares about me and my future as well as all of her clients. Thanks for making this painful process easy for me and my family!"
~Lauren

"I was struggling with making a transfer from one college to the next and had no idea how to make things happen. I was recommended to contact Gina and it was the best thing that happened to me. Not only did she take care of the transfer process, she was able to make sure that I received credits for the classes that I had already taken without having to repeat them. A very frustrating process was turned into a very exciting & easy one but only thanks to Gina. She is one of a kind and cares deeply for people. That's a rarity nowadays. I can't thank her enough."
~Ray

"All I can say is thank you, thank you, thank you. You went above and beyond what any counselor would have done for us. We will always be your number 1 fan."
~Meghan & Thomas

Get That Degree

I. MAKING THE COLLEGE LIST

College is a big investment in both your money and time, therefore, I encourage you to do as much research as possible when you consider schools you might like to attend. First, let's go over the type of schools that are out there.

Four-year colleges will award bachelor's degrees upon completion of the degree program that you choose. These colleges can be public or private and can have a certain religious affiliation, single sex attendees, or other criteria needed in order to attend. Therefore, it is important to do your research to see what meets your needs and preferences. Some schools are known as liberal arts colleges, and these schools tend to focus on undergraduate education solely, as opposed to a university which is much more diverse. Universities will offer undergraduate studies also but will have graduate, professional, and doctorate degree programs as well. There are also other four year colleges that will be specific to a certain field of study such as music, art, or religion. In order to further advance your education to attend graduate school or a professional degree, it is mandatory that you receive your bachelor's degree first. Remember that just because it's a four year college or university, it can take longer than that to complete your degree program in order to graduate. This happens for a multitude of reasons such as; availability of classes, the major you are studying, and failing or having to repeat classes.

Community colleges or Junior colleges will allow you to receive an associate's degree or a certificate, in your field of study, in two years. These schools are usually much more affordable than the four year colleges or universities. If you are undecided on your major, or there are financial constraints for not being able to attend a four year college, then this is a viable option to consider.

Trade or technical schools will allow you to receive a license, certificate, or a degree for a specific career that interests you. These schools will prepare you for a certain field such as; automotive, electrical, computer technology, culinary, dental hygienist, paralegal, medical assistance, and the list goes on. Each program will have their own set of requirements needed to complete in order to graduate, which can take from less than a year to a few years.

Lastly, many students are confused as to whether or not they should attend a private school or a public one. My opinion is that neither of these schools should be discounted solely because it's a public or private school. However, they should be discounted if the school is not the right match for you. Keep in mind that private schools will be more costly but they also have more financial aid funds to award than that of the public schools. Therefore, I reiterate, don't rule a school out over it being public or private.

Having said all of that, let's begin at the beginning which is creating a college list. I am sure you have heard that you should be categorizing colleges into three categories. 1-"Safety" schools where you will most likely be accepted, 2- "Target" schools where you are on an even level with admission criteria, and 3- the dreaded "Reach" schools which have a higher academic competitiveness. There is nothing wrong in applying to a variety of colleges, so please don't let anyone talk you out of that. It is important to look at the criteria given, but, more importantly, you need to look at the appeal of each school to your needs and wants. When researching various schools, keep in mind your answers to questions such as; is this the right size school for me, do they have academic majors that interest me, how do I like to spend my free time, or is this too far/close to home? This is a time of discovery by you, and about you, as you get to know all the preferences you may want in a college. By doing so, it will allow you to have the clarity needed to choose the schools you would like to apply to.

With over 4,000 colleges and universities (including 2 and 4 year degree granting institutions), it's imperative that you try and narrow down your choices. The internet is an amazing tool to allow you to research the various colleges, but you can also talk with your Independent College Counselor or Guidance Counselor. They have the expertise about colleges and can help you in your list building. Keep in mind that all schools will have pros and cons, and you must decide what is absolutely essential in a college along with things you can live without. I know, I know, you can live without the classes and the workload, but I promise you that won't be on my worksheet list, so keep dreaming!

Another thing to be looking at, while working on your college list, is that of affordability. This is the time when you need to talk with your parents or the financial guru of your college fund, to see what amounts are feasible or just over the top. We will discuss financial aid later on in this book which helps many people be able to enter the school of their dreams, but I tell my students that you need to have a financial plan in play with your family before your search begins. Take the time to have that conversation in order to know where you stand.

It's really important to research colleges and universities to see all that they offer on every level from academics, dorm life, dining options, to other activities. Take advantage of social media and follow the schools that interest you. By following these schools, you can see what they are up to and to hear from current students. It will serve you positively as the school will see just how interested you are which can play a factor when it comes time to submit your application. It will also give you an advantage to know why that school is the right fit for you.

There are many college online search tools to help you in your research. To begin with, many high schools are using a program called Naviance. If your high school is using this, then you will be given log in information in order to use this system. Once you establish your account with them, you can search colleges with the criteria that you specify. You can then research and save the schools that are of interest to you. This program will be a way to communicate with your guidance office also, so they know which schools you are applying to, and they can send your transcript/recommendation letters accordingly. Check with your high school to see if they use Naviance. If your school doesn't, you can still get the same results by logging on to other college search sites such as www.bigfuture.org.

Another helpful way to make your list, is by attending a college fair which are usually held in the fall or spring at various cities. At these fairs, you will be able to meet with college admission representatives from many different schools that are all together in one place to make up this college fair. These fairs can be held at your high school, a local meeting place, and/or shopping malls. The various colleges, in attendance, will be in alphabetical order and will have a table (booth) with pamphlets and information you need for selecting your list. I encourage you to ask questions to the representatives and gather as much information as possible to help in your search. If for some reason you are not able to speak with one of the representatives, then, by all means, make sure you take the pamphlets or whatever information they have at their table so you can further read about that school on your own time. The best time to attend one of these college fairs is during your junior year in high school.

Additionally, you can also meet with a college representative when they are visiting your high school. Please note that not all high schools will have this opportunity as it is impossible for admission counselors to go to every high school there is. However, if your high school sends an announcement that a certain college rep will be visiting, then take advantage of that and sign up for a visit if that is a school you would like more information about. The visits are short and you will fill out a card with your information so that you can be put on their physical mail and email list. This is a great way to stay informed.

I recommend you keep your list between 6-12 colleges and

really research those to see which schools will make the final cut, based on your preferences. Now, I am asked all the time as to how many schools should a student apply to, and the answer is that there is no exact number or science. Having said that, I recommend no more than 5 to 8 schools to send applications to with a variety of safety, target, and reach schools, if they are of interest to you.

Tips to research schools in order to compile your list:

- ❖ Go directly to college websites.
- ❖ Attend college fairs. This will give you time to speak directly with admission representatives.
- ❖ Visit the campus.
- ❖ Talk to current students.
- ❖ Email or call admission counselors with any questions you may have.

The main thing to remember is that you should apply to the schools that are your number one choices and that based on your research, you would feel comfortable attending should you be accepted. You don't have to have the exact same measurement of happiness at each of them, but it's important that you do have a good feeling of being a student at any of them.

Don't forget that you need to have your list compiled and

organized before you begin your senior year so you will be ready to send out applications when the Common Application and individual college websites have released their applications. By creating your list early, it will give you more time to research the schools to see which ones would be considered a "perfect fit" to you. I have included a worksheet at the end of this book complete with lots of questions to be asking yourself as you compile your list.

2. CAMPUS VISITS

This is the fun part of the college process when you are able to visit the various campuses to see if it's the right fit for you. It is an influential part of college planning since it allows you, the prospective student, and your family, a college tour, along with asking any questions you have to be answered from the staff and, more importantly, the current students. These visits should be used to take note of the differences & similarities between the various campuses and the uniqueness of each of them. You can learn a lot about the school you are looking at by asking questions, and please do not be afraid to speak up. That is what the tour guides are there for. The best time to begin visiting is in the spring of your junior year and the summer before your senior year.

I am often asked how many colleges should I visit, or do I

need to visit all the ones I am thinking about? My answer is to visit the ones that you are most interested in to see if you have the same interest when you are on the actual campus. As far as the number of visits to make, that's a choice between you and your family. If you don't get to visit all the campuses that you would like to apply to, then by all means don't stress over that. What you should do is after your acceptances come in, go and take a campus tour then if you weren't able to prior to that time. This can help to make your final decision. You already know that you are an accepted student, so you can visit with even more confidence.

Some tips to follow in order to have the best experience:

❖ Visit the college websites or call their admissions office to schedule a tour. Most schools have many dates and times that you can sign up for. There are some universities that make it a requirement to register for an official tour. There are also self-guided tours if you are unable to make an official one. In this case, you can go to the admissions office upon arrival at the campus, and get a map & brochure to guide you through. When you arrive, make sure you only park in the visitor parking lots.

❖ Have questions in mind. This is your time to get as much information as possible to help you make your decision when the time comes. What is it that you want to know and learn about this campus? Some thoughts...

- What academics are offered?

- What is the average size of the classes?

- Are there study abroad opportunities, honors programs, career counseling prior to graduation?

- Do the majority of students receive financial aid? Merit scholarships?

❖ Wear comfortable clothes and shoes. You will be doing a lot of walking on the tour so make sure that your feet don't pay the price because you had to be a fashionista. Dress for the appropriate weather, and bring water & snacks to have along the way.

❖ Visit a college while the semester is in session. Going to a campus while the students are there, and classes are going on, is a great way to really observe what goes on at that particular university. You can see the daily ins and outs of what the students go through. You will be able to eat in the dining hall and can also visit the various offices such as financial aid, registrar etc. It will give you a better perspective of what you will be doing should you get accepted and decide to attend that particular college.

❖ Take pictures and notes. I can't stress this enough, especially when you begin to visit many schools since you can get easily overwhelmed. For this reason, write down your thoughts, take pictures, and make notes of the pros and cons. Having this list, and talking things over with your family, will help you tremendously when making your decision.

❖ If you are interested in playing a sport, go and meet with the coach and see a game or the team practice.

❖ Read the bulletin boards while you are there also. Take note of the upcoming events or happenings at the school.

❖ Check out the library to see what that is like. Are there lots of students gathered to study together or more people just working independently? Is it a comfortable place to you if you need to go there to study?

❖ Take the time to also check out the college town and the surrounding area. What are the transportation options as well as stores or places of interest.

❖ At the end of your visit, if you have a chance to meet with a college admission counselor, then take that opportunity to introduce yourself and let them get to know about you a little bit more in depth.

As you can see, these campus visits can be extremely helpful to you in choosing the schools that you wish to apply to and later for making the decision of which school to attend. You will be able to see the various buildings such as; the dorms, dining halls, student centers, bookstores, academic halls, and athletic facilities. Being on campus will give you a feeling of what it's like to be there as a student, so I encourage you to make college visits.

You can also inquire about sitting in on a class, and some schools even allow you to stay overnight. Check with the school to see if you can take advantage of either of those options. If you are unable to go in person, for whatever reason, then visit a college website to see if they have virtual tours posted. Most now have them on their admissions page.

I have included a worksheet at the end which you can use to compare the different colleges in various categories. You may be able to use some of the categories to form your own questions when you are visiting in person. Take advantage of that worksheet to help you along in this process. There are many things that you will be taking in on your campus visit, but, above all, try to make some connections while you are there. Connect with the faculty and especially the students, since you can get some honest feedback from current students regarding their college experience at that school. It has been very beneficial for most of my students so far. Most of all, be yourself, relax, and enjoy your time there.

3. COLLEGE INTERVIEWS

An interview is a way for the college representative to get to know you better through face to face communication and more in depth than what you have put on paper. It also allows for you to discuss your reasons for wanting to attend that particular school and what it is you want to achieve there. It gives you a chance to talk further about anything in your application that may be significant for the admissions department to know, prior to making their decision, and to allot for time to ask any questions you may need answered.

Please note that an interview is not a required part of every college or university. It is necessary that you find out whether the interview is optional, required, or non-existent at each of the schools you would like to apply to. If it is a requirement, or you are given a choice, then make the arrangements to set up the interview. If the school is a far distance from your home, then coordinate to allow for the campus tour to be done on the same day.

The two different types of interviews are the informational and the evaluative. In the informational interview, you will have the chance to get more information about the college, and ask as many different questions that you need answered. This gives you the opportunity to learn as much as possible about the school. During this time, you will be able to receive much more personalized information about the various degree programs as well as extracurricular activities. This interview is widely used as the colleges way of recruiting. Use this time wisely to get as many of your questions answered as possible, but remember that you are still being evaluated by the interviewer. Make sure to continue to make a good impression.

The evaluative interview is important to the college as this is their way of better assessing you as a candidate for the upcoming freshman class. The interviewer will take notes during your conversation, and his or her evaluation of you will become a part of your application. You can still ask questions in this type of interview, although here the focus will be more on the admissions counselor trying to gain as much information about you as possible. Again, it's crucial that you make a good impression.

The biggest thing to stress when it comes to the interview is to be fully prepared. Research the school so that you can answer the questions that come up. This will show the representative that you are the right fit for that college. It will come across in your enthusiasm for the college and the programs that are available to you, so do your homework by learning as much as you can.

It's always a good idea to have some questions that you want to ask of the interviewer as that shows your interest in that college. Don't ask the typical questions that can be found answered on their website either. If you know what major you'd like to declare, then ask questions pertaining to that specific major that isn't just the basic information you can find on their website or their brochures. Delve deep to show your genuine enthusiasm for attending their university.

Some tips for the college interview:

❖ Be prepared. If there is anything in your application that you feel warrants a further explanation, then this is your chance to do so. Also, what is it that you want the interviewer to really know about you. Give that some thought ahead of time.

❖ Dress nicely and appropriately. Jeans, t-shirts, and shorts are really not acceptable attire.

❖ Be polite! Show confidence without appearing pretentious.

- ❖ Be early to your scheduled appointment time.
- ❖ Answer the questions to the best of your ability while maintaining honesty.
- ❖ Practice answering questions about yourself with a friend or family member, especially if you've never been interviewed before.
- ❖ Allow the interview to be more of a conversation. Don't go in there sounding as if you're reading off of a script.
- ❖ After the interview, you should send a thank-you email or letter to the college representative who took the time to speak with you. Respect of someone else and their time will go a long way.

When answering the questions, it is important not to just give one word answers or to talk and talk. Don't go off on tangents that aren't relative to the question. Think about your answer to each question carefully rather than to blurt something out that you might have to back track on. State your goals and your visions of attending this college, should you be accepted. This interview should be treated as a conversation, so be yourself. Use the worksheet at the end of this book to help you be prepared with some possible questions that may be asked.

4. THE COLLEGE ESSAY

The college essay is the part that my students and their parents have always stressed over the most. Although it is a very important and integral part of your application, it shouldn't cause so much grief that you fear it. Instead, embrace it, and know that this essay is your chance to let the admissions counselor get to really know who you are. Express yourself in a way that shows off your personality, beliefs, passion, and the value that only you can bring to their college or university.

When writing this essay it is critical that you focus on yourself and not to write what you think a college admissions counselor would want to hear. They want to know who YOU are and what makes you unique. Give personal details so they can really get a sense of what makes you outstanding. Your essay is your story, so make it as interesting as possible based on your life experiences and ordeals. Show them how you would be a valuable asset to their college.

There will be several topics to choose from, so find the one that best suits your interests. Choose a topic that will allow you to tell about something that is relevant to you and that has had some sort of an impact on your life. This way you can write about what's most important in a humble way. Remember, you won't get a second chance to make a first impression, so put some thought into this.

Some of my tips to ease you through this process:

❖ Start early! Don't wait until a week before your application is due and then decide it's time to throw something together. Trust me, this is a very bad idea and the cause of much stress. Also, admissions counselors have seen it all, and if they feel that you didn't take the time to put some thought and care into your personal essay, then why should they choose you.

❖ Brainstorm all ideas and thoughts. When you narrow down and choose the question you would like to write about, list all your ideas without worrying about the exact order or manner in which you are going to write the essay. This is a time to jot down thoughts and then, from there, you can simplify it to the exact points you want to make in your essay. It's much easier to make a list than to sit there staring at blank paper or a computer screen trying to come up with a way to begin. Once the ideas are listed, you can make sense of it all.

❖ Be yourself! I can't stress it enough how important it is to be who you are, and to stay true to that when you're writing. Let your personality shine through since this is your essay. I would advise against you writing in a brash tone or writing untruths. Instead, write about something that is unique to you.

❖ When choosing what topic to write about, go through all of the essay prompts and read them thoroughly. Which topic really stands out that would allow you to show the real you to the admissions counselor. That's the one you should choose.

❖ Yes, you can add humor as there is no written rule that it has to be all serious and business like. However, some people won't find your adult humor as funny as you may, especially a college admissions counselor, so make sure it's not in poor taste.

❖ Your opening statement should pack a punch. I say this because it's a sure fire way to grab the attention of the reader, so they want to read more. Try not to be standard with the opening line of; My essay is about_____. This is so boring and mundane. Rather, take the time to think of something fabulous to begin with, and continue until you finish with a powerful conclusion as well. Make sure your essay flows from beginning to end.

❖ Write your essay from your point of view. I have seen so many students write their essay from a third person point of view, and that should not be done. This is about you and what's important and meaningful to you, so use your voice! Also, be descriptive, give details, and paint a picture that the admissions counselor reading it can really grasp your individualism and uniqueness. Focus on the message you want to give.

❖ Don't just reiterate what you already said in your application. When choosing your topic to write about, make sure it is new information that you are letting the reader know about you. Do not just tell the same stuff that can be found in your application. Those are already known facts about you. Write about something that they have no knowledge of yet.

❖ When writing your essay, don't just give the admissions counselor a play by play description of an event that shaped your life or something that changed you. Instead, talk about the impact or effect it had on you. How did it change you, or what did you learn, is what you should concentrate on when you're writing. Being descriptive about the life experience is much better than a play by play.

❖ Step away from your essay for a couple of days. After you have finished your essay, take a break from it. Leave it alone for three to four days, and then go back to read it again to see if you still feel as strongly about it as you did prior. It's important to take a break from it because you will view it more clearly when you pick it up days later. Then you can see if that's the essay you want to represent you and accompany your college application.

❖ Review and proofread your essay. This is critical in the process of making sure your essay is grammatically accurate. Correct any typos and grammar mistakes before sending it in. It also is a good idea to ask a parent or a teacher to review it to see if this essay really identifies who you are to the reader, and to give you any constructive criticism that is warranted. Make sure that when someone is looking it over they don't make changes that drown out your voice. Double-check that who you are is being portrayed and not someone else's voice.

❖ Don't write an essay that will end up making the reader feel embarrassed. I know there are some personal issues that may have happened in your life that you think would make for a good essay, but if it comes at the cost of making the reader feel uneasy, then please rethink your thoughts.

❖ Don't go about bragging and trying to sell yourself in your essay. You don't need to overemphasize that you are this perfectly wonderful person and that they would be stupid not to choose you. Rather, show them in your essay about things that are meaningful to you and what you care about.

❖ Finally, please don't go over the word count. It is better to write a shorter essay than to go over the allotted words. Remember, these admissions counselors are having to read hundreds, and sometimes thousands, of essays. Therefore, it needs to stay in the word count guidelines.

Once you have completed all the steps above, ask yourself one more question and that is; "If I had a stranger read my essay, would this give them an insight into my life and/or me as a person"? If the answer is no, then go back and make any adjustments that need to be made. If the answer is yes, then pat yourself on the back and be proud of your accomplishment. You did it!

Get That Degree

5. LETTERS OF RECOMMENDATION

Most colleges and universities will ask for at least one to three letters of recommendation, therefore, this is something that can't be avoided. These recommendations are normally written by your teachers, coaches, employers, and one by your guidance counselor. They are meant to give the admissions counselors a more in depth look at who you are as a person, along with their academic assessment of you. Colleges want to hear from them since they can rely on their judgment of your character. These letters become a very important part of your application.

Here are some of my tips regarding recommendation letters:

❖ Decide on two or three teachers that you would like to write your recommendation. Ask these teachers or coaches early in the school year if they would write a letter on your behalf. I recommend giving them at least 30 days to work on your letter. Remember, they are not obligated to do this for you, so it's to your benefit to allow them enough time to put their thoughts down in writing(if they agree to write the letter). You have to respect the time they will need to complete your letter and the many other students who may ask them for one also. Ask early!

❖ Depending on the school you apply to, make sure you meet the required number of recommendation letters they are asking for. If that particular school states that no extra letters should be submitted, then make sure you follow that rule and don't send additional letters hoping that will up your chances of being accepted. It actually hinders you since it shows that you are not able to follow the rules that were set forth.

❖ Many high schools are now using a system called Naviance, which is a college readiness software provider. If your high school is using this system, then you must ask the teachers and your guidance counselor to write a letter for you through your Naviance account. Some schools require you to fill out an application through your career or guidance center in order to ask for recommendation letters. Find out as to what the rules are surrounding your high school in order to accommodate your requests for letters.

❖ Make certain that you take the time after that person has written a letter on your behalf to show them your gratitude. Send a personal thank you letter (email is acceptable) to each individual who took time out of their day to write that letter for you. This is an important step in maintaining a trait that is very highly respected.

❖ When you are completing your college applications, whether it is through Common App or the individual college websites, it is critical that you waive your rights to view the recommendation letters. This is crucial for the admissions office to know that they can trust the recommendation letters they are receiving, since you haven't seen them, thus, they will not have been tampered with.

❖ Don't assume that the people you ask to write a recommendation letter for you know all that there is to know about you. Make it easier for them by giving them a resume including any accomplishments and goals you may want them to include in their letter. You can also ask if you could spend some time talking with them, before they write the letter, to give them positive information about you.

Recommendation letters from your teachers, guidance counselors, coaches, or employers, are an extremely significant part of your college application. These letters will reveal more information about who you are as a person and the way you interact with others in whatever capacity. Think carefully before you choose who will write your letters.

Get That Degree

6. THE APPLICATION PROCESS

This chapter will explain the various admission options there are and how to make sure your application stands out. Please keep in mind that not all colleges and universities offer all of the various admission options, but, for the sake of this chapter, I will define all the options that are out there. The other significant thing to always note is that, no matter what, there are always deadlines, and if you miss a deadline, it cannot be overturned!

❖ Regular Decision – This option is used for all colleges and universities. This deadline is usually in January or February, depending on the school.

❖ Early Action – This option allows you to have an early admission process, however it is "non-binding", which allows you to decline their offer of admission if you decide you no longer want to go there. This deadline takes place in the fall of your senior year.

❖ Early Decision – This option allows you to also have an early admission process, however this is "binding", meaning you are under an obligation to enroll in that school if you are accepted. This deadline also takes place in the fall of your senior year.

❖ Rolling Admission – This option offers a longer time period for accepting applications. When your application is received, it is evaluated as it comes in (once all the necessary paperwork is received) and not like the regular decision which waits until the deadline and then reviews the candidates.

Let's further explore the early admission process so you can understand that more fully. As I said prior, Early Action is the "non-binding" option which is usually chosen by students who want to have some security that they were accepted to a certain school of their choice early on. However, this will still allow you to continue to apply to other schools without having to make a commitment right away. Therefore, if you choose this option, make sure your other applications are being completed and sent in under regular decision so that in the case of an Early Action denial, you will be prepared with other schools as your back-up. Also, the deadline for this application option is normally in the fall, beginning as early as the middle of

October, and your notification is normally sent within eight weeks.

If you choose to use the Early Decision option, which is the "binding" one, then please keep in mind that this means you will have to enroll in that school should you be accepted. The students that use this option are those that know for sure they want to attend that school and want the peace of mind knowing they are accepted early at their top pick. If you choose this option, please note that you are not allowed to apply Early Decision to any other school. If you are accepted, you are to immediately notify the other schools that you have sent applications to, in order for your applications to be withdrawn.

The other thing to keep in mind when you apply Early Decision, is that you will usually not know your financial aid information before you enroll there. Now, there are some colleges that will offer you a way out should the financial aid offer not be sufficient enough for you to be able to attend. If you go with this option and financial aid is extremely important, then it would be in your best interest to call the admissions office to see if they have an "opt out" on the basis of not enough aid for affordability. Like the Early Action option, the deadline for this application option is also in the fall, beginning as early as the middle of October, and your notification is normally sent within eight weeks.

I am asked repeatedly if I think early decision should be done. Here are some of my reasons as to when early decision is the right way to go.

* ❖ If you are certain of the school (your first choice) and know that it's the right fit for you.

* ❖ If your academic record places you in the range they are looking for.

* ❖ If you will not need your academic grades from the first half of your senior year and can submit with just your senior year first quarter grades.

* ❖ If you will be okay to attend financially based on what they will give you, or not give you, as a financial aid packet, without having to compare what other schools may offer you.

* ❖ If you will have no problem meeting their application deadline along with your test scores, essay, supplemental questions, and the needed letters of recommendation.

* ❖ If you really want to know what college you will be attending as soon as possible.

Some closing thoughts on these two options. Since their deadline is quite early in your senior year as opposed to regular decision, please be aware that you will not have much time to be able to improve your test scores or increase your GPA. Therefore, if you have decided that you are going to apply using one of these options, then it is imperative that you begin your college essay sooner than later so that you have time to fine tune it. Start your application early as well, so that you can make sure it's complete. If the school asks for other short essay questions on their application, you will still have time to complete them in a non-hurried manner. You don't want to submit a rushed application. Plan your time accordingly, and don't procrastinate.

Once you have decided on the option, it is now time to get down to the nitty gritty of the application. The most widely used application form is called the Common Application. It can be found online at ***www.commonapp.org*** and allows you to apply to any of the schools that use this application, with only one form. There is also the Universal College Application which can be found online at ***www.universalcollegeapp.com*** and is used by much less schools than the common app.

Some colleges and universities want you to apply strictly through their website, and some still want you to fill out the paper version of their application. It would take a very large book for me to tell you which school uses what form. When you are ready to apply, the individual school websites will tell you which form they accept for their applications to be submitted.

The applications will be looking for your basic information such as; your name, address, parental and family information, academic information, and any extracurricular activities, volunteer work, or jobs. Your application will require your transcript, essay, letters of recommendation, and standardized test scores. Some schools are now going test optional and it will tell you if test scores are mandatory or not. Certain colleges will also ask for supplemental short questions to be answered as well.

Some tips for filling out your application:

❖ Don't wait until the day before the deadline to fill out the applications because things can go wrong. I have had several students come to me saying they missed a deadline because the computer system was down, and they couldn't submit their application in time. They were hoping that I could call the school and ask for an extension due to technical problems, but that cannot happen. Deadlines are set, and they need to be adhered to. Start your applications early to avoid problems later.

❖ Any academic recognition you have received should be noted. This can range from awards you have been given to making the honor roll. Include all your accomplishments since your freshman year through senior year to date. This is a positive indicator to the college admissions counselor that academic success is important to you.

❖ When you list your extracurricular activities, make sure that you include any titles you may have received, any awards, and what role you actually play in that club, sport, or activity. By listing your extracurricular activities, it shows more of who you are as a person and what other qualities you have.

❖ If you volunteer, please list your contributions to your community or the area in which you volunteer, so the admissions counselor can see your level of involvement and the impact it is having. Again, this is showing a level of dedication to helping others.

❖ Any paid employment positions should include the number of hours you work per week, as well as any leadership roles or responsibilities you have been given. Employment shows a level of maturity, since you are now balancing school and work responsibly.

❖ There will be non-refundable fees per college application. Make sure you take that into consideration, as that must be paid before your application can be submitted. There are also fee waivers, so check with the particular college to see if there is a waiver available especially if those fees will be a financial hardship for you and your family.

❖ Colleges will need to have your transcript sent along with the letters of recommendation. Find out from your guidance office or career center as to what their protocol is in order to get that information sent to the various schools that you are applying to. If your school is using Naviance, then you will request those materials to be sent via your Naviance account. Again, check with your high school, and keep in mind that you are not the only student needing materials sent. Therefore, ask early once you know where you are going to send your applications to, in order for your high school administrator and counselor to prepare the materials to send on your behalf. Don't wait until the last day.

❖ If the college or university is requiring you to send SAT scores, then you will need to send the official ones. To do so, you will need to log onto *www.collegeboard.org* and request your scores to be sent to the colleges you are applying to. There will be fees associated with this. Plan accordingly as well as allotting time for your scores to be received. Official SAT scores could take as long as 2-3 weeks for the colleges to receive them. Check the college requirements so that you know if SAT scores are a requirement or optional. If they are optional, it is entirely up to you whether or not you want the admissions counselor to have them as a part of your application packet in order to make their decision.

❖ If you need ACT scores sent, then the same rules apply as SAT scores with the exception that you'll need to log onto *www.act.org* to request scores to be sent to the various colleges. ACT scores could take as long as 2-3 weeks to be received by your school. Again, check with the college requirements to see if this is required or optional to send to them.

❖ Grades matter for all 4 years that you are in high school. Continue to do well even in your senior year. Keep in mind that some schools will require you to send your mid-year senior grades and/or your final senior grades, so be cognizant of that.

❖ Using the common application is time saving, since it allows you to use that same application to any of the schools that accept that form. Each college will have their own requirements regarding supplemental essays and test scores policy, so take note. These supplemental essays are much shorter than the college essay and will have their own set of rules. Again, if it's optional to answer their questions, my opinion is that I would answer those questions because they are asking them for a reason. Usually it is more specific in order to get to know you better and to see if their college or university is a "perfect" fit. Of course it's entirely up to you as to whether or not you choose to answer them if they are optional.

❖ Ultimately, I hope you can enjoy this process as you are filling out your college applications. It is an exciting time for you and your family and by pressing the submit button when your applications are completed, it brings you one step closer to this next stage of life.

Get That Degree

7. FINANCIAL AID

This is the part of the college process that carries so many questions along with a lot of confusion, so I'll try to make this as simple as possible. Financial aid refers to grants, work-study, scholarships, and loans. Here are the different terms and definitions so that you are familiar. For this section, I will be speaking as if I were talking to a group of parents since they ultimately take care of the financial end.

Grants – This is money that is awarded that doesn't need to be paid back. These are usually awarded based on financial need.

Federal Pell Grant – This grant is provided to students from the government who show need and who have not yet earned their first bachelor's degree.

Federal Supplemental Educational Opportunity Grant (FSEOG) – Undergraduate students with exceptional financial need can receive this grant.

Teacher Education Assistance for College and Higher Education (TEACH) – This grant gives up to $4,000 each year to education majors who agree to teach in a high-need field, at an elementary or secondary school, or educational service agency that serves low-income families along with other criteria that must be met.

Scholarships – These are awarded based on merit, need, or a combination of both, and do not need to be repaid. Scholarships will have their own requirements and varying amounts.

Free Application for Federal Student Aid (FAFSA) – This is a free application in order to qualify for federal aid such as grants, work study, and loans. Colleges will require you to have this application submitted in order to be awarded financial aid.

Work Study – This is a program where the student can have a part-time campus job that is funded by the government. In order to qualify, a FAFSA form must be completed.

Loans – This is money that is borrowed with the understanding that it will need to be paid back, along with interest, over a certain period of time. You can apply for student loans and parental loans through the government (FAFSA), banks, and other private sources.

Scholarships and Grants are available from the federal and state governments, local businesses & organizations, national private organizations, corporations, and colleges/universities. The beauty of this type of financial aid is that it is "free" money, since it is never to be paid back. There are many factors that go into how this is awarded, but, normally, it is based on academic merit, athletic skill, musical ability, performing arts, certain fields of study, and/or financial need. Eligibility for this type of aid will be determined by the college financial aid office.

Please note that each college and university will have their own criteria for financial aid along with deadlines. It is necessary that you know what their requirements are. This information can be found on the individual schools website under financial aid.

The first step in securing any aid is to fill out the FAFSA (Free Application for Student Aid) online at *www.fafsa.gov*, and yes, it's a free application. This application is the single most important form that is needed in order to be considered for financial aid. The US Department of Education administers this, and it is a requirement of all colleges, universities, and technical schools if you want to have any chance at financial aid. The FAFSA is open to applicants beginning October 1st of every year. You must apply for aid every year while your student is in school full-time. The reason this must be done is due to the fact that peoples circumstances change. Incomes change, people lose jobs, marital status changes, another child in the family may be going to college, so it's mandatory to do this. This application consists of questions which ask basic information, and for the financial part it consists of questions regarding income, savings accounts, and a couple of other questions regarding assets. It is a fairly straight forward form and not too much detail.

In order to complete the FAFSA, the student and a parent will need to answer the questions fully, and then submit the application. There will need to be a signature for the parent and the child. The easiest way to submit it is with an electronic signature. You can do this by obtaining an FSA ID for each of you. In order to receive one, you need to go to **https://fsaid.ed.gov** and fill out the form. This ID will be used for signing your FAFSA application. It's essential that you write down or store the information somewhere that you can access it easily. You can also print out the signature page and send it in to the US Department of Education, if you choose not to receive an FSA ID online.

Aside from the FAFSA form, there is another application that is a requirement by approximately 400 colleges as well as some scholarship organizations, and this is called the CSS Profile (College Scholarship Service). This application is administered by College Board and is a much more extensive application. The financial questions are much more involved than those in the FAFSA. In this form, you will be asked for the value of your home, your retirement accounts, mortgage balances, when you bought your home, will any other family members be able to help pay for college, what are you planning on contributing towards college, and the list goes on. This form is not used by too many schools, but it is important to find out if your school is requiring this form in order for them to award you any type of financial aid.

The CSS Profile is one of the dreaded parts of the financial aid process that people hate doing. The reason is that it is very tedious to complete, and it delves very deeply into the parents and students financial picture. It is also not a free application as there is a cost associated with submitting this form as compared to FAFSA which is completely free to submit. As of today's date, the fee is $25.00 for the first college and any additional ones that will require the CSS, will cost $16.00 each. There are fee waivers for those who had a fee waiver for the SAT or if they are from low-income families. You can request a fee waiver for up to eight colleges.

The CSS Profile is filled out online through College Board. Yes, the same company where you registered your child for the PSAT and/or SAT. You will need their log in information to apply. The CSS Profile will give the college a very clear picture of the entire families financial situation in order for them to determine the amount of institutional aid that can be awarded to the student. These awards can be very substantial and many times make the decision of whether that student can afford to attend or not. A lot of this money comes from endowments that are given to the school by various donors. Therefore, it's necessary that you file your CSS Profile (if required), as early as possible and definitely by the deadline date. Never miss a deadline date, as money is given on a first come, first served basis.

The CSS Profile uses the Institutional Methodology and the Consensus Methodology when calculating the amount that is needed per student to attend that particular school. Unlike the FAFSA form when figuring out the financial aid to award, the CSS Profile will take into account high medical bills and other special circumstances. The student and parents income will be used together to determine family income. This method of asking so many questions such as; income of the parents, income of the student, the value of your primary residence, debts owed, assets of both the parents & the child, provides a full financial picture so that they can see the family's ability to pay for college and to make sure all awards given are fair to all families. This allows for a much clearer picture of your finances and allows for any special circumstances as well.

Another thing to note is that any asset a parent may have that is in the name of their child, IS considered a viable asset. Also, 529 plans or college savings plans are considered a parental asset. Pension assets are not allowable, or included, in the CSS Profile. On a side note, it is not expected that parents should completely empty their assets in order to send their child to college, after all having these show a sound financial picture.

When filling out the FAFSA and the CSS Profile, you will be using your income tax return from the prior-prior year (PPY), as opposed to in the past, when you only used the prior year's (PY) taxes. I know this sounds confusing but what this means is for those students that are entering college beginning with the 2018-19 school year, you will be using your income information and your child's income information from 2016 (prior-prior year) and not 2017 (prior year) as was done in the past.

After your financial aid form (FAFSA) is submitted, you will receive a Student Aid Report (SAR) which will give you the one thing you need to know the most which is the Expected Family Contribution (EFC). This number is the minimum amount that will be expected from you and your student to meet college funding. This number comes from FAFSA using the calculations from the Federal Methodology.

Once your EFC is known, the financial aid officer will use the following formula to come up with a determination of whether you will receive financial aid, and, if so, how much will be awarded. The formula is: Total Cost of Attendance − EFC = Financial Need. If your EFC is less than the cost of attending that particular college or university, then there will be a need for financial aid and a financial aid packet should be granted to you. Please note that this is just a simple formula that is widely used, but there are also other factors that schools will take into consideration when they are putting together your financial aid.

That is why it's critical to fill out the required forms with the proper income and financial information. Your EFC is the most influential number in calculating your financial aid.

In the end, financial aid determination will be made by the individual financial aid officers at the college. They will look at your entire financial snapshot along with the different applications they require, FAFSA and/or CSS Profile, to give you your financial aid award letter. You can always appeal their decision should it deem necessary.

Before I give you tips and common mistakes to avoid, here are the facts about federal student loans. These loans are awarded to students, but a FAFSA must be filed. Federal loans come in subsidized and unsubsidized forms. The subsidized loans allow for the government to cover the interest payments while you are in school full-time. Unsubsidized loan interest payments are not met by the government, however these interest payments can be deferred while you are still in school.

For dependent students, you can borrow $5,500 for your first year in college with no more than $3,500 as a subsidized loan. Your second year it increases to $6,500 with no more than $4,500 as subsidized. Your third year and beyond is $7,500 with no more than $5,500 as subsidized. The total amount that you can borrow as a dependent undergraduate student is $31,000 over all the years with no more than $23,000 as subsidized.

If you are an independent student, then the first year you can borrow $9,500 with no more than $3,500 subsidized. The second year is $10,500 with no more than $4,500 as subsidized and your third year and beyond is $12,500 with no more than $5,500 as subsidized. The total amount you can borrow as an independent undergraduate student is $57,500 over all the years with no more than $23,000 as subsidized.

For Graduate or Professional studies, you can borrow up to $20,500 in unsubsidized loans every year. However, $138,500 is the maximum you can receive as loans for all the years.

There are many common mistakes that I want you to know about so that you don't make any when it comes to the financial aid portion of college planning:

❖ FAFSA will need information about your student, and you and your spouse, when you're filling out the form. Please make sure that you are inputting the right information to correspond with parent or student, so that you don't mix up the information. I know you may think this is just common sense, but I can't tell you how many times this happens. The real importance of this is that parental assets count much less than that of the student assets. It is critical not to allow for any mistakes when documenting between the two.

❖ I can't stress enough how important it is to verify that all social security numbers and dates of birth match the right person. There have been numerous people that have come to me to say their FAFSA forms are taking too long to process due to simple errors such as these, so proofread everything that is submitted. You don't want to miss a deadline due to simple mistakes holding the process up.

❖ Do not use abbreviations or nicknames when filling out the FAFSA because they need to match the social security number with that person. If that name doesn't match, then you will need to make adjustments which will cost you time. For example, if your name is Thomas, don't use Tommy or Tom.

❖ When it comes to the income portion of the FAFSA form, give the correct numbers when they ask for adjusted gross income as well as the total taxes paid. Read each line so that you give the accurate information associated with your tax return. You can also use the IRS tax retrieval link on the FAFSA form rather than inputting the numbers yourself.

❖ When the FAFSA asks about investments you have, do NOT include your primary home as part of that amount. They don't want that amount. However, if you do have any investment properties, then that MUST be included.

❖ Retirement accounts are NOT to be disclosed on the FAFSA form, yet, through the years, clients repeatedly include this on that form. FAFSA absolutely tells you that these accounts (IRA, SEP, SIMPLE, 401K, 403B, Keogh, profit sharing, Roth IRAs, and pensions) and their values should NOT be noted anywhere.

❖ Any assets that are not in a retirement account will be included in the EFC (Expected Family Contribution) formula when the amount of aid you qualify for is being determined. These will include checking, savings, money market, CDs, stocks, bonds, real estate investments, commodities, brokerage accounts, and mutual funds.

❖ As I said previously, the CSS Profile is administered by College Board which is the same company that administers the SAT. You'll need to log on with the credentials you used when your child registered on that site to take the PSAT or SAT. Also, you will see that it says the student should fill out the Profile, but I would not allow that since this is a very involved form requiring all kinds of financial records. It would make more sense for you, the parent, to fill this out. Again, check with the college you're applying to before worrying about the need for filling out this form.

❖ For those of you that are self-employed, do not make your company have a value that is greater than it really is. What I mean by this is that if you have a company that employs fewer than 100 employees, you do not need to include your business assets thereby increasing the value of your company. Obviously, this will decrease your aid packet. Read all the notes that go along with the FAFSA before you just start putting down all the numbers associated with your company. Those assets could mean the difference between getting aid or not.

❖ Another common problem that I have seen is that too many people aren't consistent with the forms that are submitted. For example, they submit their FAFSA forms with a different set of numbers than the CSS profile. It's imperative that you include the same information on both forms (if both the FAFSA and CSS are required), because the financial aid office will absolutely see the inconsistency. This will affect the amount of financial aid they may award you. Therefore, make sure that all the numbers and information are consistent no matter which form you are filling out.

❖ When you are filling out the FAFSA form, there is a place to list all the colleges your student is applying to. It's critical that you list all the schools that he or she will or has applied to. If a school comes up that your student applies to after you submit your FAFSA, then you can go back and add that school in by making a correction on the form. The schools on that list, that you supply, will receive a copy of your FAFSA form in order to review it for financial aid purposes. Don't leave any school out. Also, after this is filed and you receive the follow up email stating that your Student Aid Report (SAR) is complete, contact the individual financial aid offices at the schools that you have included on your FAFSA, to make sure they have received the information from the Department of Education.

❖ In the case of divorced families, the parental information that should be used is the parent whom the child spends more than half of the year with. Now, please don't confuse this with the parent who is able to declare that child as their dependent for tax return purposes. Sometimes this is the same parent, but, most times, it is the other parent. For that reason, make sure you follow the FAFSA guidelines which state it is the parent who has the child for more than six months out of the year.

❖ Again, in the case of divorced families, if you are remarried, then the stepparents financial information is required on the financial forms regardless of whether he or she has any financial obligation to help with college. Their income is part of your household income, so that is why it needs to be reported. I reiterate that it doesn't obligate them to support your child.

❖ There is a checkbox on the FAFSA form to indicate if you would like to be considered for loans and work study. By all means check this box off. If you don't, your student will not be given a second look to be a candidate for these. Please understand that even if you check this box off, your child is not under any obligation to accept these awards, if they are granted any, and can decline the offer if need be.

❖ All colleges, universities, and technical schools have certain deadlines that you will not want to miss. Some of these schools award their aid on a first come, first served basis, so don't miss any deadlines.

❖ At the end of the FAFSA form you must hit the submit button in order for your information to be transmitted. Before you can do this, you must each electronically sign the application with your FSA ID (discussed previously). You also will be given an option to send the signature page in via snail mail if you choose not to get an FSA ID.

❖ After the FAFSA is submitted, the Department of Education will send you the Student Aid Report, commonly referred to as the SAR form. This is usually received via email within 2-3 days as long as the FAFSA information is all correct when submitted. Please review the SAR form, in its entirety, to make sure that all the information is accurate and no mistakes are visible. If there are any mistakes, then you need to make the corrections and re-submit as soon as possible. The SAR report includes the significant EFC number and will be sent to all the colleges that you listed on your FAFSA form. Many scholarships will ask to have a copy of the first page of your SAR report. That is why it's crucial that nothing is wrong on that report and that all the numbers are exactly proper.

❖ Finally, and my biggest tip is to file FAFSA no matter what. I hear it too many times from parents and students asking me if they have to file the form, since they don't believe they will get any financial aid at all. I always say, "how can you make that decision when you have no idea what they look for and how their decision is made? By all means, you need and should file". Don't be the judge of whether you'll get aid or not, since it doesn't cost anything to file the FAFSA form but can mean the difference between receiving something or nothing. Assuming you'll receive nothing because you think you're not eligible, could turn out to be a very costly mistake.

As I mentioned earlier, if you are not happy with your financial aid packet, you can appeal it if there are special circumstances surrounding your appeal, as most colleges do not want to negotiate a new financial aid packet. By this I mean, income changes since you filed FAFSA, an impending divorce, unemployment, taking care of an elderly relative, or unreimbursed high medical bills. If any of these are a factor in your life, then you need to write a letter to the financial aid office of the colleges that are being pursued, to see if they are able to award any more money for you to be able to attend. Be prepared to give solid evidence of any claims you are presenting in order for a new decision to be made, if warranted. This appeal absolutely needs to be made in writing and you should be most sincere about asking for a revision. Remember, there is no entitlement here no matter what the circumstances are.

Scholarships, as explained earlier, are a form of money that is not be repaid. Of course, there are the academic and athletic scholarships, but I want you to be aware that scholarships can come from your community and local organizations to help with financial need that is still unmet. The biggest thing to remember is that your student needs to pursue these scholarships since they won't come looking for him or her. Free money is out there. Have your child make a conscious effort to research scholarships and apply to as many that are relevant as possible. You can log on to ***www.fastweb.com*** and ***www.scholarships.com*** to begin searching.

Don't just rely on the internet to search for scholarships since there are many, especially local ones, that you won't know to search for. Your student should talk with family, friends, their guidance counselor, and an Independent College Counselor, as they may know of other opportunities. Check with your place of employment and those of your spouse and child, into possible scholarship opportunities as well. You won't know unless you ask.

My biggest tip is to apply to as many scholarships as possible, provided your student meets the qualifications. Have your child work on the applications and just be there if they need assistance or have questions. Don't do the applications for them. When they are working on them, make sure directions are followed exactly and the necessary documents are provided. Make note of the deadlines and meet that timetable. No late applications will ever be accepted. Also, make sure that a complete, proof read application packet is being turned in.

Information most likely needed to complete these scholarships will include; an essay, transcripts, recommendation letters, copy of your SAR or EFC report, SAT/ACT scores, and sometimes an interview will be necessary. Whatever the case is, make sure to fulfill it.

If your child is awarded any scholarships, it is vital that he or she sends a thank you letter or email to the scholarship committee or the person who sponsored him or her. They should also send a thank you to those who wrote recommendation letters on their behalf, as well as anyone who may have helped in getting that scholarship. Respect of others, as stated earlier, will go a long way.

8. ADVICE FROM COLLEGE GRADUATES

I asked several college graduates to give advice to my readers as to what they would say to students just starting the college process. I hope you will take away some meaningful guidance from the following individuals.

»»»

"If I knew then what I know now, there are many things I would choose to do-over when trying to select a college, but there are two things I would have kept the same: my major, and my choice to do multiple internships during college.

What was hard for me to figure out before college was actually trying to picture myself at the end of college; where would I want to end up? What type of job would I want? What am I expecting out of my future college to provide to me outside of just classes (for example: career counselors, resume help, tutoring, alumni network)? At the age of 17, it's nearly impossible to know the answer to these questions. And in the end, it turns out the things I was looking for in a college often weren't what I found most useful anyway. The best choices I made in college were to meet upperclassmen in my major, and to do as many internships over the course of the 8 semesters and summers to get varied experience, and ultimately, a full time job offer before even starting my senior year." Robert N., Marist College

»»»

"Ever since I was a little girl, I always aspired to help people, but I wasn't sure how I would achieve that desire. Throughout my years of schooling I always struggled academically. I would spend countless hours studying; begin projects days in advance, and sought out tutoring only to obtain a D. When senior year arrived I applied to twelve Universities, because all I received in the mail were rejection letters. I was so discouraged.

I was accepted to Western Connecticut State University as a non-matriculated student, and with that life-changing opportunity, I began to experience success in my studies with the help of friends, family, professors, and Gina Nisco. I am forever grateful for the time Gina has invested in my academia; I would not be where I am today if it wasn't for her. I have always had a heart for elderly people, and the academic and professional exposure to Social Work in Undergraduate and my Graduate Schooling at Fordham University has allowed me to improve the quality of life for so many individuals. College gives you the opportunity to pursue your passions at a higher level, and make a difference in people's lives." Lauren P., WCSU

»»

"College is a huge undertaking, and it's easy to let it overwhelm you. For someone like myself who wasn't a historically accomplished student, I initially struggled to move past this. It wasn't until I took the advice of my professors and utilized free academic clinics and tutoring centers all over campus. When I finally had a help network I was able to realize I didn't have to do everything alone. You pay a huge tuition, use the tools they provide for you!" Daniel D., WCSU

»»

"School was always something I was good at. I studied and worked hard, but it was never really a

challenge. By the time I got to college, I realized my struggle was going to be finding a reason to be there. I needed to find a passion, which is hard when you're taking general education courses. My best advice is to think more about what you want to do, rather than what career you want. Think hard about what you value, and what kind of contribution you want to make. Don't be afraid to change directions, and always trust your gut." Kayla R., WCSU

»»»

"One of the big things I learned in hindsight is to go to school when you are ready. If that is right after high school, great! But if you need a few years to see the world or even to do nothing, also great! I decided to attend college in my late 20's and it ultimately made me a better student. Having several years in the retail workforce made me appreciate why I was going to school. I tried harder. I cared more about my grades and ultimately got a better education because of it. Had I gone straight from high school I probably would have dropped out. Although I have always known what I wanted to do, I wasn't ready.

The biggest thing I have realized since I went back to school and joined my field, is that you do things by doing them. Nothing comes to you. It may seem like they did, but you need to put yourself in the places to make them happen. You can't catch a fish without a line in the water. But you need to get up early. You need to be on time. You need to work long hours. You need to work LONGER hours. You need to do things as favors. You need to be a part of it. Take action. Your dream job isn't going to call you unless you are making your presence known.

Don't let others discourage you. I wanted to be a sound engineer and work on big Hollywood movies. People told me that it is a very competitive field and there aren't a lot of jobs. My take on it was "Sure. But SOMEONE is doing that job. And if someone can do it, why can't that person be you!" Sometimes you need to dumb things down to see the other side of the coin. Lastly, get a real email address. xxJ-Bonez420@aol will surely lose you job opportunities." Jeremy E., NEiA, Boston

»»

"Going to college was always a life dream of mine. However, going through the process of narrowing down and trying to figure out what major I wanted to pursue was quite scary. I liked high school, but I knew it was time for me to get away from home. I had never been away from my parents or my family for an extended period of time, so in a way I was a bit sheltered, and I truly had no idea what I wanted to do

or where I wanted to go with my life. So I came across a small school in the small town of Rindge, New Hampshire at a college fair. I went up and visited and committed that very same day to Franklin Pierce University. I just had this feeling that it was the perfect fit for me.

My first semester was a bit of an adjustment period. I did find myself very nervous to make friends and I was a little homesick. However, I did make lots of new friends and I had a great roommate. I found that I had some trouble balancing the work for all of my classes, so my effort did slip away for some. After my first semester, I pulled myself together and learned how to better manage my time. I also made school more of a priority than I did before. The only thing that I wish I could change is to get involved in more clubs and activities because it looks really good on a resume and can really help shape you into who you are. I couldn't have done all of this without the help and support of my parents. I am eternally grateful. The most important piece of advice I could give is to make the most of your college experience. Get involved, meet new people, and find new interests/ hobbies because it is over in the blink of an eye. " Lauren S., Franklin Pierce University

»»»

"In my family there was never any discussion on if I would go to college. It was expected of me to go to college, at a prestigious school, finish in four years, and then get a job doing what I went to school for. I ended up not accomplishing any of these goals, and could not be happier that I didn't. The overwhelming pressure from my parents and family to live up to that plan is why I ended up not completing my applications in time and going to a community college right out of high school. In hindsight the amount of money I saved getting my Associates Degree and my general studies classes done at community college was a huge bonus. I then transferred to a state school picking a major that has always interested me but I never got to study. I was thrown into it and was not prepared, but I worked harder than I had before to catch up to those who had been doing it for years. Taking part in clubs and activities outside of class helped me meet the closest friends I have in my life. It took me 6 years to get my associates and bachelors, I went to community college and a state school, and currently working outside of the area I studied.

With all that being said I would not have wanted my college experience to be any different. The best advice I can give is to not let the pressure and expectations of others influence the college experience that is right for you. Everyone's timeline is different than one another, that being said still be prepared to work harder than you ever have so that you can take the most away from college." John M., WCSU

»»

"When I stepped onto Springfield College's campus I was nervous since I haven't had to make friends since kindergarten. I wasn't sure if I would be able to find my niche but within the first hour and a half I made friends that have lasted me throughout my college career! Part of college is learning that things will fall into place without your control and learning to roll with it. You may find things are not going your way but having the faith that you will make it gets you through some of the hard times.

You need to learn to say yes. Every opportunity that lies in front of you, you should take because it would lead you to so many other life changing experiences. My advisors have helped me obtain my collegiate goals whether it be getting an A in a class to traveling to Haiti! Making these relationships with peers and advisors along with just saying a simple yes allowed me to live my college experience to the fullest." Dara G., Springfield College

»»»

"My first impression of WCSU was that it felt like 13th grade. I had no desire to go there. My plan was to move out to California after high school, establish residency and after a year apply to UCLA film school. The notion of being somewhere else, particularly the West Coast was very attractive to me and felt like a whole new beginning. Instead, I stayed in Connecticut and was strongly encouraged by my girlfriend at the time to go to Western, which was in a neighboring town. Being in my backyard, living at home and commuting with a girlfriend who dormed was nothing special for me. For her, Western was a goal accomplished. For me, it was a dream denied. I soon learned that college is what you want it to be. Regardless of where you go it depends on how much you want to invest your time and energy into meeting new people, joining new groups, attending local events and bars. The absence of self-gratification, at whatever college you choose, is no one's fault but your own. College is what you make it, same in life.

There are a number of colleges, and people go to them for different reasons. The people at WCSU, at least the vast majority, go here because they just knew they needed a degree to survive in 4 years (or 5 if you go to WCSU). The students have little ambition.

Or they have much of it but not the work ethic. One of the differences I learned between WCSU and a renowned school isn't the education I got. It's the impression the university's reputation bought me. And Western bought me very little.

By being at Western, despite how hard I worked (two majors and a minor, a 3.8 GPA, former President of a media production club and being on the Dean's list for 6 semesters), when I tell people I graduated from Western it's warrants no recognition nor admiration. Ivy League schools are different. You're buying the impression you give people when you tell strangers on job applications, relatives and friends that you graduated from somewhere prestigious. It signals to them, 'Hey, this guy is going places.' I have many wonderful memories of Western including with friends, classmates, and colleagues, but I learned too late that maybe I was destined for something more and didn't work hard enough prior to college to deserve it. But like college, as in life, it's what I choose to make it and what I'm willing to work for from here. Dream big and work to make it a reality, despite where you go to school.

One of the ways you can't fail in college is by choosing not to learn in the abstract. Find a way to take what you are learning in each class and think of how to apply it to your long-term goals. Be conscious of it. Even if you have only a feint idea of what you want to do, it's ok. It's rough clay; mold it as you go. And never think you're the smartest person in the room, regardless of the setting. You can learn something from everyone. Keep your heart and mind open to new experiences." Christian G., WCSU

»»

"When it came time to start the next chapter in my life by going to college, I couldn't have been more excited and ready to leave home for the first time. I began my first year at Daniel Webster College studying game design, but as time went on I realized that it wasn't the career I wanted to pursue. Adapting to college was quite hard and not as easy as I imagined it would be. I played hockey and had an unforgettable season, and made some friends, but Daniel Webster College didn't feel like home to me. I began to realize that maybe I wasn't as ready as I believed I was. After a hard year, I made the decision to transfer to Eastern Connecticut State University.

After transferring to Eastern, I made friends with other people who had transferred in, so we were all in the same boat. I also joined the hockey team where I made friends with my new teammates and even won a championship my junior year. I started off with a computer science major and realized that my courses were extremely hard. Eventually I decided to become a business information systems major, which was a newly adapted program. I quickly developed a positive relationship with my professors and advisors who helped guide me along the way. Thankfully, Eastern became my home.

From dealing with previous difficulties adapting to college and finding my way, I want people to know that change is okay and changes in life are necessary just as they are in technology. For us to be able to figure out our passion and true path in life, it is okay to change schools and change career paths. Through my experiences, I have learned that change is for the better, and it has helped shape me into the person that I am today. The most important piece of advice I could give is to get involved with sports or clubs, develop positive relationships with peers and professors, and work hard to gain opportunities within your field. People say that college goes by so quick, but you never really understand that until you go through it yourself. Quick is an understatement, so enjoy every minute and every hardship you might endure because it will pay off more than you might understand at this moment in time." Lorenzo S., ECSU

Get That Degree

9. ADVICE AND PARTING WORDS FROM GINA

When I started out writing this book, it was to give an easy to follow plan to make the most out of this next stage of life (college), with as little stress as possible for the student and their parents. College admissions is a complex process but with the right information and help, it can be managed without the dreaded family arguments. That was and still is my intention.

Now for my advice and final words.

To you, the student.

I know that this is a very emotional time for you as you try to sort out what, where, and how you want to do things. It is a constant time of discovery as you figure out what you want to do, where you want to go to school, and how are you going to get there. Your parents are also going through this same sort of roller coaster as they too want to help you. I am going to ask you to allow them to help, but you can ask for boundaries.

Your parents should be allowed to make suggestions about colleges that you may want to research and, most definitely, allow them to go on college visits with you. They will help you to see things you might miss and also ask questions that you might not have thought of. Remember, they want the best for you and want to help with whatever they can. If you need to set boundaries so that you are not feeling like you are being smothered, then you need to be an adult and have a conversation with them stating your intentions. Arguing should not be part of that conversation but rather a plan should come into play as to how they can help you. Don't shut them out. Sending a child to school is a bittersweet moment for your parents as well as for you. Just saying "thank you" will mean a lot to them as you move forward in this process.

Another thing to keep in mind is that it's real easy to get lost in all of the paperwork that is needed, along with keeping track of all the critical deadlines. Therefore, you need to be extremely organized. Make a list of all the deadline dates as well as syncing those dates into your calendar, and keep copies of everything you send in. It is crucial to never let a deadline pass you by since these dates will not get extended to you for any reason. Which brings me to the main point which is do not procrastinate. As I have stated several times in this book, start early. Don't wait and put things off to the last minute. The problem with that is minutes turn into hours, into days, into weeks, into months, and inevitably, something gets left to the wayside. Don't let that happen, and to avoid it, I reiterate, start early and stay away from procrastination.

The goal during this time is to enjoy the process and try to stay as stress free as possible. Although there is a lot to do, if you plan accordingly, everything will get done properly and on time. Simultaneously, while all of this is going on, make sure that you are enjoying your last year of high school. Even though you are busy with college applications and everything else that goes along with that, don't neglect your senior year. Continue to take the time to make high school memories and to have some fun.

When all of this is done, and you have made the decision of where you will be attending, take a deep breath, and celebrate you. Make sure to thank your parents, family, friends, teachers, counselors, and anyone else who has helped you during this time. Acknowledge those by showing your gratitude and love. Being respectful, as I mentioned earlier, goes a long way. Well done and Congratulations!

To you, the parents.

This time of life can be very exciting, stressful, and bittersweet for all of you. I have had many parents tell me, through the years, that if they could do it over again, they would be more supportive instead of pushy and allow their child to make their own decisions. I know this is hard to see your child for what he or she really is. For the first time, they are getting ready to go out on their own and to make critical decisions that will affect their future. Your natural instinct is to protect them and guide them, but when your direction is much different than theirs, it's important that you allow them to speak so that you can understand what they are thinking. Obviously, if it's something way out of line or not feasible for you financially, then you need to make sure they hear all that you're thinking as well. Be realistic with them. By opening up this line of communication, it will allow for honest thoughts to flow from both you and your child in order to have a better understanding of, "where do we go from here".

As far as the colleges that are being chosen by your child, don't negate them because you feel they are inadequate or you think your son/daughter has to attend an ivy league school in order to have a great future. These thoughts are far from the truth. Your child has to feel comfortable attending that college, and if they don't want an ivy league or another prestigious school, then don't put that added pressure on them. There are a lot of schools out there that will allow your child to receive a great higher education and a future after that, without it being a "brand name". I do agree that you should help with the research of schools, especially on the financial portion, but if it's a school that meets your child's criteria and your budget, then it's important to support his or her decision.

When it comes time to go to the college visits, I think you should attend with your child. You can be another set of eyes along with listening to the advantages and disadvantages of that particular school. Don't take a front seat however, and by this I mean, have your child choose the schools he or she would like to visit. Your job is to be a supportive role in this stage of the game.

When the acceptance letters and/or the denial letters come in, it is of utmost importance to be there to celebrate their wins and losses. Let them know how proud you are of their acceptances (celebrate) and for the losses, let them know this isn't the end of the world (share their pain). College admissions is full of uncertainty, so don't allow that to break your child down. There are far bigger problems in life, and that is your role to teach them that.

Decision day is a big relief for your child since they can finally feel they have a plan for their future education goals. Along the lines of advice that I gave to your child, take a deep breath, make sure you tell your son or daughter how proud you are of them, and show them your love. Celebrate this next stage of life and all the emotions you are and will be feeling. You know far too well how fast the time goes.

However, before you know it, they will be back home raiding your fridge and wanting their laundry done. I guess that's another book for another day.

☺☺☺☺☺☺☺☺☺☺☺☺☺☺☺☺☺☺☺☺☺☺☺☺☺☺☺☺☺☺☺☺☺☺

10. WORKSHEETS

COLLEGE SELECTION QUESTIONNAIRE

What is really important to you? The following questions can help you narrow down your preferences in choosing colleges to apply to.

What goals do I have for my higher education?

_____

_____

_____

_____

What is my GPA, class rank, test scores?

_____

_____

_____

_____

What would I like to major in? (It's fine to be undecided)

_____

_____

_____

_____

How will this college help me to obtain my goals?

_____

_____

_____

_____

What academic opportunities would I like to take advantage of? (Study Abroad, Internships)

_____

_____

_____

_____

What about extracurricular events? (clubs, sports, fraternities or sororities)

_____

_____

_____

_____

PREP QUESTIONS FOR YOUR INTERVIEW

Fill this out prior to your interview so that you are prepared
for these possible questions

How do you like your high school, and what has been the
most positive and most negative thing about it?

_____

_____

_____

_____

What has been a significant contribution you have made to
your high school?

_____

_____

_____

_____

What are your future goals?

_____

_____

_____

_____

What do you like about this college?

_____

_____

_____

_____

What is or was your favorite subject in high school and why?

_____

_____

_____

_____

What do you do in your free time?

_____

_____

_____

_____

Tell me some things about you that I don't see in your application?

_____

_____

_____

_____

There are many qualified candidates that have applied to get into our school. What sets you apart from the other students?

_____

_____

_____

What are you hoping to achieve, besides a degree, while attending our university?

Are there any events that have shaped your life either negatively or positively?

Who or what has had the biggest impact on you?

Tell me the accomplishments that you are most proud of?

QUESTIONS TO ASK DURING YOUR COLLEGE VISIT OR INTERVIEW

WHAT IS THE AVERAGE SIZE OF YOUR CLASSES?

WHAT IS THE CORE CURRICULUM?

WHAT ARE THE MOST POPULAR MAJORS?

WHEN DO I HAVE TO DECLARE A MAJOR? A MINOR?

ARE THERE INTERNSHIP OPPORTUNITIES THAT YOU HELP STUDENTS WITH?

DO YOU HELP WITH GETTING A JOB AFTER GRADUATION?

HOW DO I GET AN ON CAMPUS JOB?

ARE SOME DORMS BETTER THAN OTHERS?

HOW DO WE SELECT ROOMS AND ROOMMATES?

WHAT CAN YOU TELL ME ABOUT OFF CAMPUS HOUSING?

ARE THERE A LOT OF STUDENTS WHO LIVE OFF CAMPUS AND WHY?

ARE DORMS CLOSED DURING WINTER OR SPRING BREAKS OR HOLIDAYS?

WHAT IS SOMETHING THAT STUDENTS COMPLAIN ABOUT REGARDING THIS CAMPUS?

WHAT IS SOMETHING THAT STUDENTS LOVE ABOUT THIS CAMPUS?

WHAT ARE SOME CHALLENGES OF THIS COLLEGE?

ASK A STUDENT, IF THEY HAD A CHOICE, WOULD THEY STAY AT THIS COLLEGE OR TRANSFER SOMEWHERE ELSE? WHY?

ASK QUESTIONS OF THE VARIOUS ACADEMIC DEPARTMENTS THAT INTEREST YOU TO GET MORE INFORMATION.

WHAT ARE THE EXTRACURRICULAR ACTIVITIES OFFERED?

WHAT ABOUT CAMPUS SAFETY?

WHAT IS THE POLICY ON HAVING FRIENDS COME VISIT ME AND CAN THEY STAY OVER IN MY DORM?

QUESTIONS OR THOUGHTS YOU CAN THINK OF.

_____

_____

_____

_____

_____

_____

_____

_____

_____

_____

_____

_____

_____

_____

_____

_____

_____

_____

_____

_____

_____

COLLEGE COMPARISON WORKSHEET

COMPARE THE DIFFERENT COLLEGES YOU ARE DECIDING
ON IN ORDER TO GAIN CLARITY ON CHOOSING THE
SCHOOLS YOU WOULD LIKE TO APPLY TO.

COLLEGE NAME			
SIZE OF CAMPUS			
DISTANCE FROM HOME			
SIZE OF CITY/TOWN			
STUDENT POPULATION			
RELIGIOUS AFFILIATION			
2 AND/OR 4 YEAR DEGREES			
MAJOR/MINORS OFFERED THAT INTEREST YOU			
CLUBS OR ORGANIZATIONS THAT INTEREST YOU			
ATHLETICS OFFERED			
FRATERNITIES OR SORORITIES			

ACADEMIC HELP RESOURCES			
RESIDENCE HALL LIFE – SPECIAL REQUIREMENTS			
DINING HALL OPTIONS			
ADMISSION DEADLINES			
SAT OR ACT REQUIRED			
AVERAGE GPA & TEST SCORES OF ACCEPTED STUDENTS			
IS THIS A "SAFETY" OR A "REACH"SCHOOL			
FINANCIAL AID DEADLINES			
CSS REQUIRED			
WHAT SCHOLARSHIPS ARE AWARDED BY THIS SCHOOL			
TUITION & FEES			
ROOM & BOARD			
BOOKS/SUPPLIES			

MISC SUPPLIES			
TRANSPORTATION			
APPLICATION FEES			
OVERALL IMPRESSIONS			
RANK YOUR COLLEGE CHOICES			

COLLEGE COSTS CALCULATIONS

USE THIS WORKSHEET TO DETERMINE THE COSTS OF
ATTENDING AND TO SEE HOW MUCH YOU WILL NEED TO PAY

COLLEGE NAME			
TUITION & FEES			
ROOM AND BOARD			
BOOKS & SCHOOL SUPPLIES			
HEALTH INSURANCE FEE			
ANY OTHER FEES			
TOTAL CHARGES			

SCHOLARSHIPS AND GRANTS RECEIVED

COLLEGE NAME			
FEDERAL PELL GRANT			
STATE GRANT			
COLLEGE GRANT			
SEOG GRANT			
TEACH GRANT			
COLLEGE SCHOLARSHIP			
PRIVATE OUTSIDE SCHOLARSHIPS			
TOTAL RECEIVED			

SAVINGS AND FAMILY CONTRIBUTIONS

COLLEGE NAME			
529 PLAN			
PARENTS CONTRIBUTION			
STUDENTS CONTRIBUTION			
OTHER'S CONTRIBUTION			
TOTAL CONTRIBUTIONS			

STUDENT AND PRIVATE LOANS

COLLEGE NAME			
PERKINS LOAN			
FEDERAL SUBSIDIZED LOAN			
FEDERAL UNSUBSIDIZED LOAN			
FEDERAL PLUS LOAN			
STATE STUDENT LOAN			
PRIVATE LOAN			
TOTAL LOANS			

SUMMARY

COLLEGE NAME			
TOTAL CHARGES			
TOTAL RECEIVED			
TOTAL CONTRIBUTIONS			
TOTAL LOANS			
UNMET COSTS			

D'Amore-Nisco

Tear This Dorm Checklist Out To Shop With

Bedding:

☐ Mattress Topper

☐ Mattress Pad

☐ 2 Sets of Bed Sheets

☐ Extra Pillowcases

☐ Comforter

☐ Pillows

☐ Blanket

Bathroom Products and Toiletries:

☐ Shower Caddy

☐ Shampoo & Conditioner

☐ Body Wash

☐ Razors

☐ Towels

☐ Shower Shoes

☐ Deodorant

☐ Shaving Cream

- ☐ Lotion
- ☐ Toothbrush
- ☐ Toothpaste
- ☐ Dental Floss
- ☐ Mouthwash
- ☐ Q-tips & Cotton Balls
- ☐ Hairbrush
- ☐ Hair Products
- ☐ Nail Clippers
- ☐ Tissues
- ☐ Band-Aids & Neosporin
- ☐ Ibuprofen/Tylenol, Vitamins
- ☐ Daily Medications
- ☐ Hair Dryer/Straightener

Laundry Items:

- ☐ Detergent
- ☐ Dryer Sheets
- ☐ Stain Remover
- ☐ Hangers

☐ Laundry Basket/Hamper

Desk Items:

☐ Ethernet Cable

☐ Laptop & Charger

☐ Printer/Paper/Ink

☐ Flash Drive

☐ Surge Protector

☐ Extension Cords

☐ Desk Lamp

☐ Chair Cushion for Desk Chair

☐ Organizer for Desk Drawer

☐ Stapler & Staples

☐ Scissors

☐ Notebooks

☐ Highlighters

☐ Paper Clips

☐ Scotch Tape

☐ Pens & Pencils

☐ Binders

☐ Permanent Markers

☐ Thumbtacks

☐ Dry-Erase Board

☐ Cork Board

Cleaning Items:

☐ Paper Towels

☐ Dish Detergent (small bottle)

☐ Clorox Wipes

☐ Vacuum

Miscellaneous:

☐ Paper Plates, Plastic Cups, Utensils, & Bowls

☐ Refrigerator/Microwave (check with your college to see about renting these appliances)

☐ Ziploc Bags

☐ Storage Containers

☐ Snack Bin to keep snacks in

☐ Clip Chips

☐ Backpack

☐ TV, Gaming System

☐ Phone Charger

☐ Posters/Pictures for your walls

☐ First Aid Kit

☐ Area Rug

☐ Fan

☐ Under the Bed Bins

☐ Garbage Can & Liners

☐ Can Opener

☐ Safe or Trunk with a Lock

Glossary

Academic Year
Colleges and Universities consist of 2 semesters (Fall & Spring).

Accrued Interest
This is interest that is accumulating on the unpaid portion of your loans.

ACT
College entrance exam based on what students learn in high school. This standardized multiple choice test will consist of English, math, science, and reading. There is also an optional essay section.

Admission Tests
These tests are to evaluate a student's readiness for college level work along with their skills. The 2 standardized tests are known as the SAT and the ACT.

Admission Deferral
Your application will be reconsidered at a later date along with a decision.

Advanced Placement
These are college equivalent courses that are taken in high school and if the student passes a test, will be awarded college credit.

Amortization
Paying off your debt with a fixed repayment schedule in regular installments that consist of principal and interest.

Annual Percentage Rate (APR)
This is the percentage rate of your loans that represent the annual cost of borrowing that money.

Associate Degree
This degree is granted by the college after completing a two-year course of study.

Award Letter
This letter will inform you of the financial aid that is being offered to you along with the amounts per semester and the types of aid you are awarded. It will let you know the deadlines for accepting the awards and how you are to do so.

Bachelor's Degree
This degree is granted by the college or university after completing a four or five year course of study.

Bursar
A college official that is responsible for payments and billing. This will include tuition, fees, room & board, and other miscellaneous expenses.

Candidates Reply Date Agreement (CRDA)
This is an agreement sponsored by the National Association for College Admission Counseling, **where it allows students to have until May 1 in order to accept or decline a college offer of admission.**

Class Rank
This is a number that is determined by a measurement of your academic achievement compared with the other students in your grade.

College Application Essay
The essay that is submitted as part of your college application which is also known as your personal statement.

College Credit
This is what you will receive when you complete and pass a college course. Every major will have a certain number of credits that you will need to achieve in order to graduate.

Common Application
A standard college application that can be used by many colleges and universities.

Consolidation
The act of combining all of your student loans into a single loan.

Cost of Attendance

This is the total amount of all expenses in order to attend that particular school prior to receiving any financial aid. This will include tuition, fees, room & board, books, supplies, health insurance (if you have none), and living expenses.

CSS/Financial Aid PROFILE®

The CSS (College Scholarship Service) is offered through College Board and is a financial aid application much more extensive than the FAFSA. This form is used by more than 400 colleges, universities, and some private scholarship organizations in order to award financial aid money.

Default

When you fail to make a payment on your loan or meet the terms of your loan as stated when you signed the promissory note. Defaulted loans are usually sent to a collection agency or an attorney to have them collect the money that is owed.

Deferment

A temporary postponement of repaying your monthly loan. Student loan deferments are granted to students as long as they remain a full time student.

Delinquent

When you are not making loan payments on time or not meeting the terms of the promissory note, then you will be delinquent on your payments which can add additional late fees and charges to your loan. This will also affect your credit.

Demonstrated Need
This is the difference between the total cost of attendance and your EFC (expected family contribution).

Disbursement
This is when your loan lender sends or releases the money to your school or to the borrower.

Disclosure Statement
The document that shows the actual cost and all the terms, including the interest & fees, of your loans.

Early Action (EA)
This option allows you to submit your application before the regular deadline date to receive an early admission decision. However, it is "non-binding" which allows you to decline their offer of admission if you decide you no longer want to go there.

Early Decision (ED)
This option allows you to submit your application to your first-choice college before the regular deadline date. However, this is "binding" which means you are under an obligation to enroll in that school if you are accepted.

Enrollment Status
This refers to whether you are full-time or part-time and is based on the number of classes/credit hours you are taking each semester.

Equal Credit Opportunity Act
This law was established by the federal government stating that lenders are prohibited from any discrimination based on race,

religion, color, national origin, sex, age, marital status, or participation in any and all public assistance programs.

Expected Family Contribution (EFC)
This is a number that colleges will use when they are determining your financial aid award packet. It is a calculation based on the information that you supply on your FAFSA form regarding your family's financial picture.

Federal Direct Student Loan
Subsidized and Unsubsidized loans that are awarded to students through the federal government based on need.

Federal Direct Student Loan Program
This is the loan program where the federal government is the lender but the school manages the funds.

Federal Methodology
This is a need analysis formula that was established by Congress, and is used to calculate your family's expected financial contribution towards college, university, or a technical school.

Federal Pell Grant
A federal grant that is awarded to undergraduate students who demonstrate financial need.

Federal Supplemental Educational Opportunity Grant (FSEOG)
A grant that is awarded by the individual school financial aid offices to those who are the neediest. Not all schools participate in this program.

Financial Aid
Money that is given to you in the forms of grants, work-study, scholarships, or money that is loaned to you in the form of government or private loans.

Free Application for Federal Student Aid (FAFSA)
FAFSA is a free application that you need to submit in order to receive any federal money for aid. Most colleges and universities require this in order to receive federal grants, work study, and loans.

Full-time Student
You must be enrolled as an undergraduate for at least 12 credit hours each semester to be considered full-time.

Grade Point Average (GPA)
This number represents your overall academic performance and is calculated by a point value system that is assigned to each grade that you earn.

Grant
This is money that is awarded that doesn't need to be paid back. These are usually awarded based on financial need.

Independent Student
A student that as of January 1st of the academic year is at least 24 years of age and is only reporting his/her income when applying for financial aid. Also, if you are under 24, you are considered an independent student if you are not claimed as a dependent on your parents previous year's tax return, an orphan or a ward of the state, a graduate student, a veteran of

the US Armed Forces, or if you are a supporter of a legal dependent. Please note that a student can't just legally declare independence due to the fact that one's parents are not helping with the cost of their education.

Legacy Applicant
Colleges will ask you on your application if a relative (parent, grandparent, or sibling) is a graduate of that particular school, since some schools will give preference to you if that is the case.

Loan
This is money that is borrowed with the understanding that it will need to be paid back, along with interest, over a certain period of time. You can apply for student loans through the government (FAFSA), banks, and other private sources.

Master Promissory Note
When you borrow money (loans) under the federal loan programs, you, the student, must sign this form. Once this form is signed, it will carry through for all your academic years that you are receiving loans, without having to sign one every year.

Merit Aid
Money awarded to students for successful personal achievements. Scholarships are considered merit aid.

Need-Blind Admission
Admission decisions are made without any consideration of the financial circumstance surrounding the applicant.

Net Price
This is the actual, true amount that a student will pay to attend a particular college or university.

Net Price Calculator
This is an online tool that gives you a personalized estimate of the cost to attend a certain college. College websites will have a link that you can click to their net price calculator.

Open Admission
A college will accept any high school graduate regardless of their GPA, until they are able to fill all the spaces needed for the upcoming class. Community colleges generally have an open admission policy.

Origination Fee
This fee is used for the administering of a loan and is normally paid by the borrower to the lender.

Outside Scholarship
These scholarships are awarded by private organizations, businesses, and individuals. They are also known as private scholarships since they are not given from the college or the federal government.

Part-time Student
When you are enrolled as an undergraduate with fewer than 12 credit hours each semester.

Placement Tests
Tests that will help to determine what level courses you are ready for or if it would be more beneficial to take a remedial course in English and/or math on a college level.

PLUS Loan
This federal loan is made available to parents of dependent undergraduate students in order to help pay for their child's college or career school. A graduate or professional student is also eligible for a PLUS loan.

Priority Date or Deadline
Dates assigned whereby your application (admission, financial aid, housing) must be submitted in order to be considered. Do not miss a deadline date.

Promissory Note
This is a legal and binding document which states all the terms and conditions of the loan you are taking out. All borrowers are required to sign this note before any of the loan funds can be dispersed.

Registrar
A college official who is in charge of registering students along with maintaining your permanent college records.

Reserve Officers' Training Corps (ROTC)
This program will be a combination of college classes along with military training as you work on your bachelor's degree. ROTC does offer scholarships to those students agreeing to be a part of the military after graduation.

Residency Requirements

In order to receive in-state tuition, you must be a resident of that particular state for a certain amount of time. The eligibility requirements can be found on the individual college websites.

Rolling Admission

This option isn't one that you choose but rather it's the way the school continues to receive applications. With this, your application is evaluated as it comes in (once all the necessary paperwork is received) and not like the regular decision which waits until the deadline and then reviews the candidates.

SAT

College admission test which is administered by College Board that consists of reading, math, and writing. The writing portion will include you to do a written essay in order to be evaluated.

SAT Subject Tests

College admission tests that are subject specific in English, math, science, history, and languages. They run an hour long to complete.

Satisfactory Academic Progress (SAP)

In order to continue to receive any federal financial aid, you must be progressing satisfactorily in college. Each college will have their own policy as to what is considered satisfactory.

Scholarship

These are awarded based on merit, need, or a combination of both and do not need to be repaid. Scholarships will have their own requirements and varying amounts.

State Grant

Money that is awarded to the student from the state in which he or she resides and does not need to be repaid.

Student Aid Report (SAR)

After the FAFSA (Free Application for Federal Student Aid) is submitted, you will receive a report that will let you know what your EFC (expected family contribution) is. This is called your SAR and will be needed for financial aid and also many scholarships will require a copy of it.

Subsidized Direct Loan

While the student is in school full time or has a loan deferment, the federal government will pay the accrued interest on their federal student loan.

Transcript

An official record of all of your class or course work in school and college. In order to apply to college, you will need to submit your high school transcript.

Transfer Student

A student who enrolls in a different college after completing at least one semester at another college or university.

Undergraduate Student

A college student working on their bachelor's or associate's degree.

Verification

This is a process that the schools will use to verify the accuracy of the information that you submitted on your FAFSA form. You can be asked to submit a copy of your signed tax returns (both student and parent) as well as other documents they deem necessary.

Waiting List

Colleges defer your admission decision until they hear from all the accepted students as to whether they are going to accept or decline their offer. If there are empty spots left, colleges can then fill those spots with students off of the waiting list if they choose to.

Weighted Grade Point Average (WGPA)

This number represents your overall academic performance and is calculated by a higher point value system that is assigned to each grade that you earn in more difficult classes such as AP or Honors.

Work-Study

This is a program where the student can have a part-time campus job which is funded by the government. In order to qualify, a FAFSA form must be completed.

ABOUT THE AUTHOR

For as long as she can remember, Gina has always had an overwhelming desire to help people with their life's journey! Her college education background is in Psychology which has allowed her to delve deeper into how the brain works which, in turn, gives her a better understanding of how we can "make or break" life.

Gina is a published Author of the book, Positive Next Steps, and a Public Speaker on topics relating to living your best life! She has been interviewed for several online publications and has also been a guest on WTNH Channel 8 CT Style. She is a Certified Public Speaker, Certified Life Strategies and Stress Management Counselor, Independent College Counselor, Divorce Mediator, Certified Corporate Wellness Coach, and Certified Results Counselor!

Gina is a true optimist full of enthusiasm and an Entrepreneur who is the Founder and President of Positive Next Steps; a company thriving on helping people achieve their best life possible! **Positive Next Steps was founded on the principle to help others continue telling their story as they live their purpose, or if it's time to rewrite one's story, then she can provide you with the necessary steps. Gina's company was built with such passion to teach you that commitment and confidence will bring about possibilities.**

As you can see, her experience in a multitude of fields has one very common theme and that is helping others find their true potential. She believes that we are all complex individuals and it is her obligation to be as educated and well-versed in the areas of our life that can be thrown off balance.

Gina assists parents and their children with the entire college process and helps others set a plan to reach their life goals. She is a leader in her field and will continue to assist those who want to live the life they imagined! Gina M. D'Amore-Nisco is available for speaking engagements, consultations, and workshops. Details will be sent upon request. To contact Gina, you can email her at gina@collegeplanadvisors.com

Thoughts

Thoughts_____

_____

_____

_____

_____

_____

_____

_____

_____

_____

_____

_____

_____

_____

_____

_____

_____

_____

Thoughts_____

_____

_____

_____

_____

_____

_____

_____

_____

_____

_____

_____

_____

_____

_____

_____

_____

Thoughts_____

_____

_____

_____

_____

_____

_____

_____

_____

_____

_____

_____

_____

_____

_____

_____

_____

_____

D'Amore-Nisco

Congratulations on this next chapter in your life.

Enjoy the journey today and always.

www.ingramcontent.com/pod-product-compliance
Lightning Source LLC
Chambersburg PA
CBHW060904280326
41934CB00007B/1179